HEALTHY CHOICES

GETTING ALONG WITH OTHERS

Cath Senker

PowerKiDS press
New York

Text copyright © Cath Senker 2004
The right of Cath Senker to be identified as the author of this Work has been asserted by her in accordance with the Copyright, Designs, and Patents Act 1988

Published in 2008 by The Rosen Publishing Group, Inc.
29 East 21st Street, New York, NY 10010

Copyright © 2008 Wayland/The Rosen Publishing Group, Inc.

All rights reserved. No part of this book may be reproduced in any form without permission from the publisher, except by a reviewer.

First Edition

Consultant: Jayne Wright
Design: Sarah Borny

The publishers would like to thank the following for allowing us to reproduce their pictures in this book:
Hodder Wayland Picture Library; 4, 5, 6, 7, 8, 9, 10, 11, 13, 14 15, 16, 17, 18, 19, 20, 21 / Zul Mukhida; 12

Library of Congress Cataloging-in-Publication Data

Senker, Cath.
  Getting along with others / Cath Senker. — 1st ed.
      p. cm. — (Healthy choices)
  Includes index.
  ISBN 978-1-4042-4301-9 (library binding)
 1. Interpersonal relations in children. 2. Social interaction in children. 3. Social learning. 4. Parent and child. 5. Questions and answers. I. Title.
  BF723.I646S46 2008
  158.2'5—dc22
                                        2007032800

Manufactured in China

Contents

What kinds of family are there? 4

Why do I have to share my things? 6

Why do I have to straighten up? 8

Why do I have to listen? 10

Why are we moving to a new house? 12

How can I help the new boy? 14

Why do other kids pick on me? 16

Why did Grandpa die? 18

What can I do when I feel sad? 20

Glossary and index 22

Finding out more 24

What kinds of family are there?

There are lots of different kinds! Many kids live with Mom and Dad. But sometimes moms and dads don't get along any more, and decide to live in different homes.

Maybe your mom or dad lives with somebody else now. Maybe you live with different people, too. You might have a **stepmother** or stepfather, or stepsisters and stepbrothers.

Maybe you live just with Mom or just with Dad, or even Grandma and Grandpa. Sometimes babysitters look after kids. All families have some things in common. They are people who live together and try to care for each other.

How many different kinds of family do you know? What's the same and what's different about how they live?

Why do I have to share my things?

 Sharing is kind. If you share, it shows you care. It means you are thinking about other people. It's a friendly thing to do. People will like you and want to play with you if you share your things with them.

Which things can you share with your brother, sister, or friend? Which things can't you share, and why?

Do you ever feel **jealous**? You might be jealous of your brother or sister. Maybe they were given great new toys for their birthday, and you want to play with them.

Remember—it's not right to fight. If you share your toys, others will share their toys with you. When you share your things, you can have more fun together.

Why do I have to straighten up?

Straightening up is helpful. As you get older, you can do more things for yourself. You can straigthen your own room and help wash the dishes. You can take care of pets.

Smaller children and older people might like your help, too. Helping people is very grown up and it makes you feel good.

If you help other people, they'll be happier to help you. Just think—if you help Dad wash the car, he'll have more time to play a game with you or read you a story.

How do you help at home? Who helps you each day?

Why do I have to listen?

"Pick up the phone! Leave that alone!" Adults often have to tell you important things. They may need your help. Sometimes they might call to warn you about **danger**.

It's horrible when people don't listen to you. It makes you feel small and not important. You don't want to make other people feel like that, do you? Take turns to listen and talk. You'll find out interesting things and hear some new ideas.

Can you think of a time when you didn't listen and something bad happened?

If you have an argument, listen to the other person. You might understand why they have a different *opinion*.

Why are we moving to a new house?

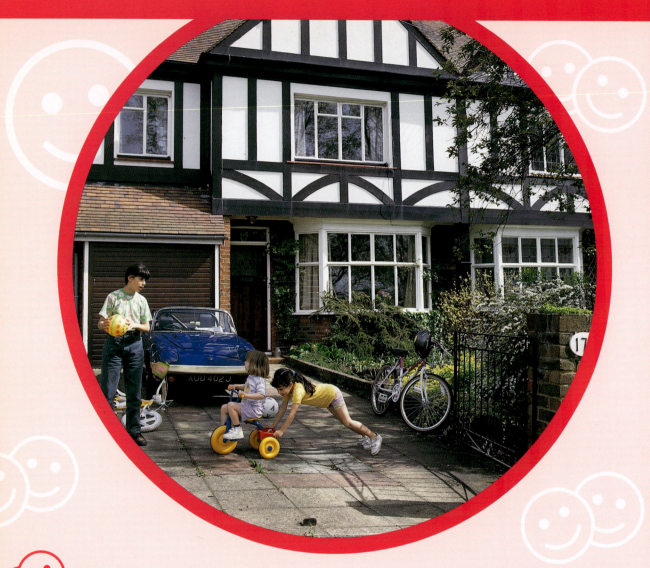

There are many reasons for moving to a new house. Maybe a parent has a new job in a different place. You might be moving to a home with a little more space.

You may have to go to a new school and get to know new people. You might feel shy—it's easy to see why. You will deal with the change, and you will learn to become more **confident.** It might take a little time. Don't worry—you will soon settle down and make new friends.

Have you ever moved to a new place? What did it feel like?

How can I help the new boy?

 Talk to him and get to know him! It's good to get to know new people. They probably know some exciting games and interesting things.

At recess, be kind—don't leave him behind! You can show the new boy around the school. Why not ask him to play your game? At lunchtime, you can invite him to sit with you and your friends.

Think about how you would feel if it was your first day at school. What would you like others to do to make you feel welcome and comfortable?

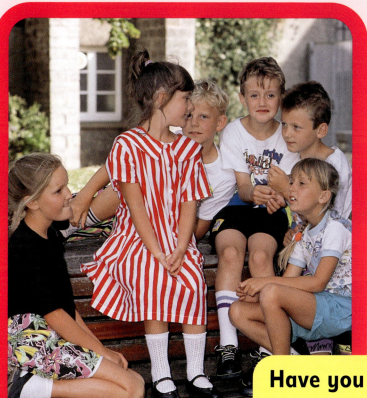

Say, "What's your name? Want to play our game?"

Have you had a new child in your class, and how did you welcome him or her?

Why do other kids pick on me?

Some children hurt other children or make them feel sad on purpose. They are **bullies**. Bullies hurt others, because it makes them feel "big." Maybe they have their own problems to figure out.

How do you think it feels to be bullied?

Teachers need to know if children keep upsetting or hurting you. They will talk to the bullies and help them to understand why it is wrong to hurt other kids.

It is important to tell an adult if you are being picked on. Bullies pick on all kinds of children, for many different reasons. Remember—it is not your fault if you have done nothing to annoy them.

Why did Grandpa die?

When people get very old, they die. Occasionally, they die younger because they are sick or have an accident.

When someone dies, it is normal to feel very sad. You might even feel angry with them for dying, because they are not there for you any more. It's fine to show you are unhappy.

It's better to talk about it than to keep quiet and be miserable inside. You might want to look at pictures of the person to remember them.

Do you know anyone who has died, or have you had a pet that died? How do you feel now?

What can I do when I feel sad?

 Everyone feels sad sometimes. If you are sad because of a problem, it's good to talk to your friends or family. It's fine to cry and let out your feelings.

Try to find things to do that make you feel better. Spending some time on your own may help. You could do a drawing or a painting to show how you feel inside.

How about listening to your favorite music or watching a movie? Playing sports is great, too. Running around releases **chemicals** in your body that make you feel happier.

Glossary and index

bullies 16 — People who frighten or hurt other people on purpose.

babysitters 5 — If your parents can't look after you, you might be taken care of by another adult who is a babysitter.

chemicals 21 — Substances inside your body that can affect the way you feel.

confident 13 — Feeling sure of yourself.

danger 10 — When something is not safe.

jealous 7 — Feeling unhappy because you want something that someone else has.

opinion 11 — What someone thinks about something.

sharing 6, 7 — Letting someone else use something that is yours.

stepmother 4 — The woman who is married to your father but who is not your real mother.

Finding out more

Books to read:

Cheat (Good and Bad)
by Janine Amos
(Evans Brothers, 2007)

Go Away! (Good Friends)
by Janine Amos
(Cherrytree Books, 2003)

I'm Sorry (Good Manners)
by Janine Amos
(Cherrytree Books, 2005)

*It Won't Work!
(Good Friends)*
by Janine Amos
(Cherrytree Books, 2003)

Selfish (Good and Bad)
by Janine Amos
(Evans Brothers, 2007)

Why Be Unfriendly?
by Janine Amos
(Evans Brothers, 2007)

Why Should I Help?
by Claire Llewellyn
and Mike Gordon
(Barron's Educational, 2005)

Why Should I Listen?
by Claire Llewellyn
and Mike Gordon
(Barron's Educational, 2005)

Why Should I Share?
by Claire Llewellyn
and Mike Gordon
(Barron's Educational, 2005)

Web Sites

Due to the changing nature of Internet links, PowerKids Press has developed an online list of Web sites related to the subject of this book. This site is regularly updated. Please use this link to access this list:
www.powerkidslinks.com/health/getalong